Bullying

...ions and Feelings About ...

W
FRANKLIN WATTS
LONDON • SYDNEY

Louise Spilsbury

Illustrated by Ximena Jeria

Franklin Watts
First published in Great Britain in 2018 by The Watts Publishing Group

Copyright © The Watts Publishing Group, 2018

Editor: Melanie Palmer
Design: Lisa Peacock
Author: Louise Spilsbury

ISBN: 978 1 4451 6440 3 (Hbk)
ISBN: 978 1 4451 6441 0 (Pbk)

Printed in China

MIX
Paper from
responsible sources
FSC® C104740
FSC
www.fsc.org

Franklin Watts
An imprint of
Hachette Children's Group
Part of The Watts Publishing Group
Carmelite House
50 Victoria Embankment
London EC4Y 0DZ

An Hachette UK Company
www.hachette.co.uk

www.franklinwatts.co.uk

Bullying

Questions and Feelings About ...

Most people get along well, most of the time.
They are kind to each other and treat each
other fairly.

Why is it important to be kind?

Some people are not kind. They do and say things to make other people feel sad, scared, embarrassed or angry. This is bullying.

Bullies usually say or do mean things to hurt or upset people on purpose. They behave unkindly, often more than once.

It is not bullying if a friend is rude when you argue or if someone hurts you by mistake and they say sorry afterwards.

Some bullies tease people or call them bad names. They say mean things about a person to hurt their feelings.

Bullies who use words to mock or taunt
sometimes say they are only joking.
But bullying is never, ever funny.

*How does it feel to be called
a bad name?*

Some bullies push, pinch, kick or hit people.
They might do this to hurt or scare someone
whenever they get the chance.

Bullies may also take someone's belongings.
They may threaten to hurt that person if they
don't do what the bully wants.

Some bullies try to persuade or bully other people to gang up on one person. A bully might try to leave a person out of games, parties, or outings.

How do you think it
feels to be left out
of a game or group?

Bullies may also send nasty messages via a mobile phone or computer. A bully may post information, photos or videos about a person online to hurt or embarrass them. This is called cyberbullying.

It is particularly bad because bullies can send horrible messages at any time to reach people anywhere.

When someone is bullied it can make them feel very lonely. They can feel as if no one likes them, even though that's not true.

They might stop sleeping, eating properly, doing school work and having fun.
They might even feel so sad that they get sick.

If you are bullied the most important thing
to do is tell an adult. There are many
people who will listen and help.

You could tell a parent, a relative or a teacher. If you find it hard to talk about, you could write it in a letter.

Who do you talk to when you need help with a problem?

It's not a good idea to fight back if someone hits you. Try not to call a bully names if they insult you. The bully could get nastier and you could get into trouble, too.

Just tell an adult about the bullying. Adults can make the bullying stop.

21

Bullying is a problem that can happen to anyone.
If someone is bullied it is never their fault.

A bully might pick on something a person does or says, or the way they look. That is just an excuse. A bully just wants to be a bully.

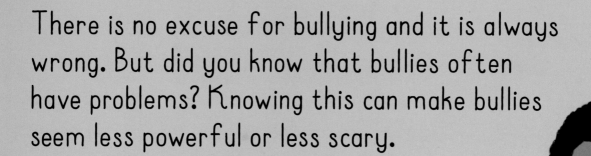

There is no excuse for bullying and it is always wrong. But did you know that bullies often have problems? Knowing this can make bullies seem less powerful or less scary.

Some bullies have problems
at home and have been bullied
themselves.

Or they could lack
confidence. Bullies often
hurt others to try to make
themselves feel bigger
or better.

Bullying is bad for everyone, even the bully. But bullies can change. They can stop being unkind and unfair.

Bullies can get help to sort out their problems.
They can learn to be kind. They can say sorry.

*How do you feel after
saying sorry for doing
something wrong?*

What would you say or do to cheer someone up?

We can all help to stop bullying. We can not join in or laugh with a bully, or we can ask an adult to stop the bully. Be kind and friendly to anyone who has been bullied so they do not feel alone.

We should all treat other people as we would like to be treated and think about other people's feelings. That way we will all feel happy and cared for!

Notes for parents and teachers

This book can be a useful way for families and professionals to start a discussion with children about bullying. Bullying can have a serious and damaging effect on children in the short- and long-term, so it's vital to help children talk about bullying.

Young people who are bullied may not always tell adults, as they may be afraid or ashamed. It's important to help children understand what bullying is, what different forms it can take and what can be done to stop it. Children can be confused about bullying and think falling out with a friend is bullying. Help them to understand that when someone says or does something intentionally hurtful and they keep doing it – even when you tell them to stop or show them that you're upset – it is bullying.

Being open and discussing bullying can help children to deal with it. Knowing that adults take bullying seriously and will listen to a child's problems makes it far more likely that children will report bullying. Talking about bullying calmly and sensibly also shows a child that's the best way to take action. It helps children to understand that while a child being bullied needs support and bullies need to be stopped, a child who bullies others can also be helped to make better choices in the future. Talking about bullying is a chance to discuss empathy and to teach children how to treat other people fairly and kindly and to think about how their actions impact others.

Classroom or Group activities:

1. Hold a session talking about how people should treat each other with respect. Let the children create their own set of rules about behaving fairly and kindly.

2. In order to encourage children to celebrate differences, choose pairs of children who don't usually play or sit together. Each pair should ask each other questions such as: what games or foods do you like? what do you do really well? what do you like best in a friend? The pairs should write three answers on a paper plate and display them.

3. Ask children to create an anti-bullying poster to raise awareness of the issue in school. They could illustrate it with signs such as a hand held up in a stop gesture or a picture of a child telling a teacher.

4. Ask children to write a story about a bullying incident and how it was resolved. The children (or an adult) could read out the stories and the children could discuss how the stories make them feel.

Further Information

Books

Giraffe is Left Out – A book about feeling bullied by Sue Graves and Trevor Dunton (Franklin Watts, 2016)
Stop Picking on Me: A First Look ay Bullying by Pat Thomas and Lesley Harker (Wayland, 2000)
The New Kid by Marie Louise Fitzpatrick (Hodder Children's, 2015)
We're all Wonders by R. J. Palacio (Puffin, 2017)

Websites

www.bullying.co.uk
www.nationalbullyinghelpline.co.uk
www.childline.org.uk/info-advice/bullying-abuse-safety/types-bullying/
www.bullyingnoway.gov.au (Australia)